WHY AR OUR BLACK MALE STUDENT– ATHLETES?

BY

SHAWN R. HAWKINS,
Businessman and Author

WHY ARE WE LOSING OUR BLACK MALE STUDENT–ATHLETES?

BY

SHAWN R. HAWKINS,
Businessman and Author

www.bookstandpublishing.com

Published by
Bookstand Publishing
Morgan Hill, CA 95037
3609_7

Note: The picture on the first title page and the front cover is of Shawn
R. Hawkins, Number 21, winning the Hampton High School Football
State Championship in 1978.
We were #1.

ISBN 978-1-61863-209-8

Printed in the United States of America

DEDICATIONS AND ACKNOWLEDGEMENTS

I Dedicate this Book To:

My sons Shawn II, Michael, and Brandon

My loving mother Ivey

My father Joseph

My aunt Doris

My sister Jodi

My cousin Jimmy

My uncle George

My nieces Jamette, Mikaela, Corbyn, and Doris

My half-brother CJ

My business partner Carla

My friends.

All of my past coaches, teachers, and mentors, who

gave up their time in helping me grow.

My family's love and support have made me the

man that I am today.

Above all, I give praise to God for everything He has

done and is still doing in my life.

God is the main reason that I am still alive to make a

difference in the lives of others.

"No weapon that is formed against me shall

prosper."

— Isaiah 54:17

TABLE OF CONTENTS

Dedications and Acknowledgements............................ v

Introduction.. ix

Chapter 1, The Black Male Student-Athlete:
Alphabetical List of Sports that Have
College Scholarship Possibilities........................... 1

Chapter 2, The Black Male Student-Athlete:
Member Institutions that Offer College
Scholarships and Financial Aid 5

Chapter 3, The Black Male Student-Athlete:
Academics... 7

Chapter 4, The Black Male Student-Athlete:
Academics and Elementary School 9

Chapter 5, The Black Male Student-Athlete:
Academics and Middle School 13

Chapter 6, The Black Male Student-Athlete:
Academics and High School................................. 17

Chapter 7, The Black Male Student-Athlete:
Academics and a College Degree 23

Words of Wisdom.. 25

Conclusion 27

About the Author 29

This Black Male Student-Athlete's Picture
Says It All 43

INTRODUCTION

The Problem

My reason for writing about the Black Male Student-Athlete is because he has the highest high school drop-out rate.

Most Black Males drop out of high school by the tenth grade.

Our Black Male Student-Athletes are not prepared academically at an early age to complete high school and college eligibility requirements, receive scholarships, attend college, and earn degrees.

The formula for resolving this situation is:

Black Male + Student-Athlete + Sports + Academics +
Elementary School + Middle School +
High School Graduate + College Scholarship +

College Graduate = College Degree

+ Bonus: A Professional Athlete with a College Degree

Today

Black Male Student-Athletes start playing sports at a very young age, from three to six years of age. These athletes participate in organized, coached sports for such organizations as the following:

- Amateur Athletic Union (AAU)

- Boys & Girls Clubs

- Youth/Pee Wee Leagues

- Recreation Leagues

I want to make an important point up front and early: Coaches coach; it is not their job to get your son or grandson into college. The responsibility for this rests upon whom? That's right, it rests upon YOU.

x

But don't worry. Through this book, I will help you to do so.

This book outlines why starting children out in academics at an early age is just as important as starting them out early in sports.

In particular, this book provides the Black Male Student-Athlete with a how-to approach to academics.

The Black Male Student-Athlete picks a sport, or two or three, at an early age.

However, the Black Male Student-Athlete must also receive help with his academics at the same early age.

It is just that simple.

Or is it?

Attention Parents, grandparents, and guardians. Let's take a look…inside.

While sports are staying the same, academics are becoming increasingly more difficult, making it harder today for the Black Male Student-Athlete to graduate from high school with a diploma, let alone get into and out of college with a degree.

So…What can be done about this? Read on.

CHAPTER 1

THE BLACK MALE STUDENT-ATHLETE: ALPHABETICAL LIST OF SPORTS THAT HAVE COLLEGE SCHOLARSHIP POSSIBILITIES

Most Black Male Student-Athletes grow up thinking that college sports are all about football, basketball, and baseball.

But the truth is that there are many sports in which Black Male Student-Athletes can participate, all of which offer college scholarship opportunities:

- Archery
- Badminton
- Baseball
- Basketball
- Bowling

- Boxing

- Cheerleading

- Cross Country

- Diving

- Equestrian

- Fencing

- Field Hockey

- Football

- Golf

- Gymnastics

- Handball

- Ice Hockey

- Indoor Track

- Judo

- Karate

- Lacrosse

- Riflery

- Rodeo

- Rowing

- Rugby

- Skiing, Cross-Country

- Skiing, Downhill

- Soccer

- Softball

- Squash

- Swimming and Diving

- Synchronized Swimming

- Tennis

- Track & Field

- Volleyball

- Water Polo

- Wrestling

What a list!

CHAPTER 2

THE BLACK MALE STUDENT-ATHLETE: MEMBER INSTITUTIONS THAT OFFER COLLEGE SCHOLARSHIPS AND FINANCIAL AID

There are several organizations, connected to two- and four-year colleges and universities, through which the Black Male Student-Athlete may obtain a college scholarship, and, in turn, attend and finish college with a degree.

Each organization has its own eligibility requirements that the Black Male Student-Athlete must meet in order to be accepted to receive a scholarship. See the graphic on the next page.

The National Collegiate Athletic Association
(**NCAA**) (4-year schools),
    Division I-A, Division I-AA
    Division II
    Division III

The National Association of Intercollegiate
Athletics (**NAIA**) (4-year schools)

The National Junior College Athletic
Association (**NJCAA**) (2-year schools)

The National Christian College Athletic
Association (**NCCAA**) (4-year schools)

CHAPTER 3

THE BLACK MALE STUDENT-ATHLETE:
ACADEMICS

It starts now! Let's build an Academic Foundation/Plan now. It doesn't matter whether you are in:

- Elementary School

- Middle School

- High School

- (Public or Private) and/or

- College

College coaches are recruiting the Black Male Student-Athlete who has what? You've got it: GOOD GRADES!

Don't pretend that your academics are good if they are not. You are just fooling yourself. This will only last for a little while. The truth will set you free.

There is no such thing as a so-called DUMB JOCK!!!

Why not? Because I am going to guide you, step by step, away from being a dumb jock!

So let's move on to the chapters that apply to the different grades and ages.

CHAPTER 4

THE BLACK MALE STUDENT-ATHLETE: ACADEMICS AND ELEMENTARY SCHOOL

Let's start with Elementary school.

The Black Male Student-Athlete in this category is between the ages of eight and ten, and is in the second through fifth grades.

Attention parents, grandparents, and guardians: See to it that your child, as a student, focuses on any or all of the following academic assistance as needed or required:

- Receives tutoring in all subjects such as English, Math, Science, etc.
- Attends writing workshops
- Attends reading workshops

- Attends test-taking workshops

- Attends workshops that teach how to learn

- Attends mentoring group sessions

- Attends summer youth camps that offer both academics and sports

- Meets with teachers to review their report cards in order to bring bad grades up to good grades

- Meets with academic advisors, if they are available

Note: Yes, you may have to pay for these services, but trust me, the costs are much less than paying for college.

Attention: It is at this time, young black male, that your sports career will begin, so you should choose a sport, or two or three, from the list in Chapter 1.

Remember: Our focus here is on obtaining a college sports scholarship.

It starts…NOW!

CHAPTER 5

THE BLACK MALE STUDENT-ATHLETE: ACADEMICS AND MIDDLE SCHOOL

Let's move on to Middle school.

The Black Male Student-Athlete is between eleven and thirteen years old, and is attending the sixth through eighth grades.

Attention parents, grandparents, and guardians: See to it that your child, as a student, focuses on any or all of the following academic assistance as needed or required. This includes everything listed in Chapter 4, plus the following:

- Receives Practice Scholastic Aptitude Test (SAT) strategy assistance

- Receives Practice American College Test (ACT) strategy assistance

Attention: It is at this time, young black male, that you should choose a sport, or two or three, from the list in Chapter 1, plus do the following:

- Attend a college eligibility requirement workshop to learn the rules and sixteen core courses that will keep you in the game.

- Attend college sports camps

Note: Again, these services will have costs, but they will be much less than the costs for college.

Remember: Our focus here is on obtaining a college sports scholarship.

At this point, you are almost in high school!

CHAPTER 6

THE BLACK MALE STUDENT-ATHLETE: ACADEMICS AND HIGH SCHOOL

Let's move on to high school.

Here the Black Male Student-Athlete is between the ages of fourteen and eighteen, and is in the ninth through twelfth grades.

It is important to know that college recruitment starts in the ninth grade. With that said, now is the time that you must make very GOOD GRADES. Every A and B grade on your transcript is important. You must maintain good grades for eight semesters.

Attention parents, grandparents, and guardians: Your Black Male Student-Athlete should focus on obtaining the academic assistance listed in Chapter 5, as needed or required, plus the following:

- Take the Scholastic Aptitude Test (SAT) Exam AND the American College Test (ACT) Exam. That's right, both. The Black Male Student-Athlete must achieve high scores on the SAT and/or ACT.

- Use the Internet to conduct research on sports scholarships. Trust me, there are plenty of them out there.

- Meet with guidance counselors. The Black Male Student-Athlete must make sure that he is on track in meeting the college eligibility requirements and the sixteen core courses

- Maintain a good GPA and Core GPA from the ninth through twelfth grades

Attention: It is at this time, young black male, that you should choose a sport, or two or three, from the list in Chapter 1, plus do the following:

- Email college coaches in all of your chosen sports to let them know that you are interested in their programs

- Send college coaches your game schedule or schedules

- Send college coaches your sports resume

- Send college coaches a videotape showing your varsity sports highlights

- Obtain assistance with the college sports recruiting process

- Work hard to earn a sports scholarship prior to the twelfth grade

- Fill out the Free Application for Federal Student Aid (FASA)

- Use tutoring and mentoring services as required for all subjects

- Obtain personal training and nutrition assistance

- Obtain help in interviewing skills

- Register for the NCAA and NAIA Eligibility Center/Clearinghouse (see page 6). In doing so, either pay the fee or get a fee waiver.

- Attend one-day and one-week college sports camps

- Ask the college coaches if they have a scholarship to offer you, and, if so, how much it is

- Go on your five official college face-to-face paid visits

- Give a verbal commitment

- Sign your National Letter of Intent

- Graduate from high school

- Send your final transcript to the clearinghouse in order to receive a sports scholarship

Note: Again, you will have to pay for these services, but they are much less than the costs for college, which is just around the corner.

Remember: Our goal here was to obtain a College Sports Scholarship.

Did you get one? GREAT!

You are almost in college now!

CHAPTER 7

THE BLACK MALE STUDENT-ATHLETE: ACADEMICS AND A COLLEGE DEGREE

Okay, you are now in college on a sports scholarship.

You made it!

God Bless You!

So now: What is your focus as a Black Male Student-Athlete in college? Here we go…

As a Student:

- You must pick a major

- You must get a Masters Degree, or a Ph.D. like former NBA player Shaquille "Shaq" O'Neil.

- You must understand the Academic

Progress Rate (APR) new requirements for incoming freshmen student-athletes

- You must continue to make good grades in order to stay in the game. *(Not making good grades could cost you your sports scholarship. You have worked too hard and spent too much money to lose your scholarship.)*

As an Athlete:

- You must earn a college degree

- You must make no excuses whatsoever

- If you happen to make it to the professional sports level, make sure you have a college degree in hand. This way, you will have something to fall back on when your playing days are over.

WORDS OF WISDOM

Ability – Is what you are capable of doing.

* * * * *

Motivation – Determines what you do.

* * * * *

Attitude – Determines how well you do it.

* * * * *

"Take control of your own life; don't wait for someone else to do it for you."

* * * * *

"No one can take that College Education from you."

* * * * *

"Making good grades helps student-athletes stay in the game."

* * * * *

"You are never too old or too young to learn."

* * * * *

"Read, Read, Read a sports book, newspaper or

magazine."

* * * * *

"To play any sport in College you must first know

the rules."

* * * * *

"Playing sports builds teamwork, leadership, trust,

self-confidence, character and muscles."

* * * * *

"The more you learn, the more you earn."

CONCLUSION

My passion, arising from God, is to help the Black Male Student-Athlete.

Being a Black Male Student-Athlete is very difficult without someone guiding them.

To be a successful Black Male Student-Athlete requires two things: Being a student FIRST and an athlete SECOND.

Never forget that both academics and sports go hand in hand towards achieving your goal of receiving a college sports scholarship and earning a college degree.

In order to achieve this goal, **academics** must start at an early age.

As a Black Male Student-Athlete, you have the right to succeed in the game of life.

Thank you and God Bless!

ABOUT THE AUTHOR

Shawn R. Hawkins is a native of Hampton, Virginia. He is a former high school student-athlete in the sports of football and basketball. He received a dual scholarship in 1978, which he turned down to focus on academics because the Department of Defense, the Navy, was looking for African-American engineers at the time.

He earned his Bachelor's degree in Electrical Engineering from Prairie View A&M University, Prairie View, Texas. Shawn continued his education and obtained two Masters degrees, one in Management, from The University of Maryland, College Park, Maryland; and the second in National

Resource Strategy, from Industrial College of Armed Forces, Fort McNair Washington, DC.

Shawn worked for the federal government for 31 years and retired in 2011 as a program manager. Shawn has also been a member of the *Kappa Alpha Psi* Fraternity, Inc., since the fall of 1980.

In Shawn's words:

"I have a passion to help student-athletes, because I had a son, Michael Hawkins, in a private high school, who was an excellent football player. At 6'2" and 315 pounds, he played offensive and defensive tackle.

"During his senior year, he got caught up in politics with his high school coach, and as a result was not recruited to play football at the college level.

He had the athletic talent, the good grades, and the SAT test score to play NCAA Division I football. However, he finished playing high school football without a scholarship to play at the collegiate level.

"I could not believe it, and felt that maybe I had overlooked some things concerning him; this was because I was going through a difficult time during his senior year.

"I knew I had to do something to help him, so I started by making his video highlight recruiting DVD, creating his sports resume, and writing a recruiting letter to send to college. Although he did not receive the Division I scholarship, he did receive a full scholarship to play football at the NCAA Division II collegiate level.

"In 2010, Michael graduated from college with a degree in Education.

"After helping my son, other parents started asking me to help them get their children athletic scholarships so that their children could play at the college level.

"The Spirit pressed me to develop a high school sports recruiting service to prevent what happened to my son from happening to others; and that is how Write to Succeed, a for-profit company, got started in 2003. God took what happened to my son and turned it around for the good of many. The company's primary service was to put together video highlight sports DVDs for future student-athletes in the ninth through twelfth grades so that they would have a product displaying their high school athletic skills to send to college coaches, increasing the possibility of their being recruited as student-athletes.

"Later, my concern was that student-athletes and parents did not understand the recruiting process concerning athletics as well as their children's academics. I felt that it was necessary to inform families about the sports recruiting process before their children reached the ninth grade.

"As a result, after the birth of Write to Succeed, God birthed World Academic Sports Team, Incorporated, a 501(c)(3) Nonprofit organization founded in May 2010. WAST is designed to assist student-athletes in successfully obtaining academic or athletic scholarships in order to help make their dreams a reality.

"Less than 6% of all high school student-athletes will go on to earn an athletic scholarship to play in college. Far fewer, less than 0.5%, will go on to play professionally. This is a startling reality for the thousands of students who, each year, fail in their attempts to use their athletic abilities to fuel their futures. Given this, the importance of academic preparedness for the future success of student-athletes is significant. The mission of WAST is to enrich, educate, and promote scholarship opportunities, both academic and athletic, for student-athletes, which will prepare them to compete in college sports. Our goal is to ensure and promote student-athletes who have a strong emphasis on academics FIRST and athletics SECOND.

"WAST conducts academic enrichment camps along with eligibility workshops for student-athletes in cities around the world, throughout the school year. The primary services include informing student-athletes in the second through twelfth grades about the rules, regulations, and athletic and academic criteria for playing college athletics.

"It is the desire of the organization to keep all services free to the student-athletes, which often means utilizing my own personal financial resources. However, it is worth it when I see student-athletes reach their desired goals.

"God has always been in my life. As an example of this, in 2001, I was going through a divorce while working at the Pentagon at the time. My son was in the tenth grade and I felt like my life was falling apart. On September 10, 2001, my son helped me to move into my apartment, and afterwards I was physically exhausted. The next morning, September 11, 2001, I called into the office to take the day off because I was still tired from moving. Later that day, I turned on the TV and saw that a plane had crashed into the Pentagon, not too far from the area where I worked. God spared my life that day, and I knew that I had a greater purpose.

"Maybe God chose me to help children receive college sports scholarships. My son graduated from high school in 2003; and from that time to the time of this writing, 2012, I have helped more than seventy-five student-athletes get into college on athletic scholarships. I plan to help many more do the same.

"The impact of starting Write to Succeed has been one of my greatest passions, because I get to see the student-athletes mature in their sports from year to year. It is also fulfilling to see the excitement and joy, of both the parents and the student-athlete, when the athlete receives a collegiate sports scholarship due to the efforts of my Write to Succeed organization. The look on their faces is priceless.

"Even more, Write to Succeed paved the way for World Academic Sports Team, Inc. The experience really changed how I view life. Although my situation at the time did not look promising, God refocused me and had me help others in a way that I had not expected. Now I want every student-athlete, under the care of our services, to achieve their dream of receiving a sports scholarship to college to help them prepare for life. We are utilizing the sports as a vehicle to help the student-athletes achieve their greater purpose, their preparation for life and their future contributions to society, so that one day they can make a difference in the lives of others.

"Both of my services, Write to Succeed and World Academic Sports Team, Inc., have impacted the lives of many student-athletes both athletically and academically. These organizations equip student-athletes with the knowledge that they need concerning the athletic recruiting process. Student-athletes are starting to realize the importance of being successful in the classroom as well as in their sports. It is emphasized and enforced that the athletic sports scholarship is the vehicle to financially pay for college, but the purpose is to achieve academically so they can earn their college degree.

"You must love God first and let Him guide you concerning each student-athlete. It is important to have a passion for helping children achieve their goal of earning a collegiate athletic scholarship, which takes mentoring student-athletes both in academics and athletics.

"There are many ways to get involved, and your donations can help assist the global vision of World Academic Sports Team, Incorporated, which is a 501(c)(3) Nonprofit organization.

"At the present time, we are welcoming donations and looking for grant opportunities to build a Sports Academy for student-athletes in grades nine through twelve. The purpose of the facility will be to prepare student-athletes academically as well as athletically so that they will be successful in the classroom as well as on the court or field. It will also provide employment opportunities for educators. The financial donations would also defray the costs of mailing out athletic recruiting packages and highlight DVDs on the behalf of the student-athletes; seminar printing for the academic enrichment camps and eligibility workshops; and possible facility costs for seminars, camps, and workshops."

All donations can be sent to Shawn R. Hawkins, P.O. Box 8630-M, Guilford Road #103, Columbia, Maryland 21046-2654.

For grant referrals or to assist the program, please contact Shawn at writetosucceed@aol.com. He looks forward to hearing from you concerning his global vision to help others.

THIS BLACK MALE STUDENT-ATHLETE'S PICTURE SAYS IT ALL

Darrell Stuckey.
(Photo by Ashleigh Lee, Copyright © *The University Daily Kansan*)

Coming to the University of Kansas on a full-ride athletic scholarship, Darrell Stuckey had two goals: Earn a college degree, and play well enough to make it to the NFL.

He was able to accomplish both.

CPSIA information can be obtained
at www.ICGtesting.com
Printed in the USA
BVOW11s0208090617
486471BV00005B/22/P